Kids'
Silliest
Riddles

Jacqueline Horsfall
Illustrated by Buck Jones

Sterling Publishing Co., Inc.
New York

For Jakob

Library of Congress Cataloging-in-Publication Data Available

10   9   8   7   6   5   4   3   2

First paperback edition published in 2003 by
Sterling Publishing Co., Inc.
387 Park Avenue South, New York, N.Y. 10016
© 2002 by Jacqueline Horsfall
Distributed in Canada by Sterling Publishing
c/o Canadian Manda Group, One Atlantic Avenue, Suite 105
Toronto, Ontario, Canada M6K 3E7
Distributed in Great Britain and Europe by Chris Lloyd
at Orca Book Services, Stanley House, Fleets Lane, Poole BH15 3AJ, England
Distributed in Australia by Capricorn Link (Australia) Pty. Ltd.
P.O. Box 704, Windsor, NSW 2756 Australia

Printed in China

Sterling ISBN 1-4027-0005-9 Hardcover

1-4027-0808-4 Paperback

Contents

1. Picnic Pranks

Why can't ants hold down their jobs?
They're always at picnics.

What kind of picnics do dentists have?
Toothpick-nics.

Why should you bring TV dinners to a picnic?
They're the best meals you ever thaw.

What do cats carry to picnics?
Mice chests.

What's the best animal to take along on a picnic?
An anteater.

Why aren't squirrels welcome at picnics?
They keep hiding the do-nuts.

Why couldn't the Cow Who Jumped Over the Moon
eat her potato salad?
The dish ran away with the spoon.

Why did the truck driver stop on the highway to eat
his potato salad?
He saw a fork in the road.

How did Yankee Doodle get mayo in his hair?
He stuck a feather in his hat and called it macaroni salad.

What does Michael Jordan store his cole slaw and potato salad in?

Basket bowls.

GRILL-A MY DREAMS

What does Dracula grill at a picnic?
Stake.

What does Zorro grill at a picnic?
Sword-fish.

What does an animal keeper grill at a picnic?
Zoo-chini.

What does a lumberjack grill at a picnic?
Chops.

What does an angel grill at a picnic?
Wings.

What does a skeleton grill at a picnic?
Ribs.

What should you use to keep tomatoes from falling out of your picnic basket?

Tomato paste.

Why did Silly Billy and Silly Sarah remove their sunhats?

They wanted baked beans.

Why did the jar of mustard burst out crying during the race?

It couldn't ketchup.

Why can't pickles sleep at a picnic?

Their covers are on too tight.

What do Japanese people put in their lemonade?

Rice cubes.

Which baseball player is great at pouring lemonade?

The pitcher.

What do bees put into your soda can first?
Their bee-hinds.

Why should you recycle empty soda cans?
Soda trash cans won't overflow.

What kind of soda do trees drink?
Root beer.

What kind of snack do astronauts take on picnics?
Space-chips.

What did the pepper say to the salt?
"Shake, pal."

BITE ME

What do mosquitoes learn in art class?
How to draw blood.

How did the mosquito become a movie star?
It passed the screen test.

What do you call a mosquito riding on your arm?
An itch-hiker.

What do you call a mosquito that sits on
your arm for 24 hours?
An all-day sucker.

What should you do if you can't stand Swiss cheese on your burger?

Just eat the holes and leave the cheese on your plate.

How do you introduce your hamburger at a picnic?

"Everyone . . . meat patty."

Why can't vegetarians have a barbecue?

The beans keep falling through the grill.

Who steals meat off the grill?

Hamburglars and dog snatchers.

What do cows put on their hot dogs?

Moo-stard.

How do you make a hot dog roll?

Say "Roll over, Spot."

When Silly Sarah sat at the picnic table, why did she shoo the flies?

She didn't want them to go barefoot.

Why did Silly Billy put bandages on his bread?

Because it had cold cuts.

When do you stop at green and go at red?

When you're eating a watermelon.

2. Monkeyshine

What's the first thing a gorilla learns at school?
His Ape-B-Cs.

What kind of ape lives in a gym?
A gympanzee.

Where do purple monkeys rule the world?
On the Planet of the Grapes.

What kind of monkey can fly?
A hot-air baboon.

What happened to the wild pig that broke out of the zoo?

They put it in hamcuffs.

Who is a pig's favorite relative?

Its oink-ul.

What lizard wears a hairpiece?

A wiguana.

What kind of bikes do polar bears ride?

Ice-cycles.

What kind of bear loves to play in the rain?
A drizzly bear.

Why do elephants have tusks?
They can't afford braces.

What did the grapes say when an elephant stepped on them?
Nothing. They just gave a little wine.

Why do elephants have wrinkled skin?
It's too hard to iron.

What has a long neck that smells good?
A giraffodil.

Why is it so cheap to feed a giraffe?
A little food goes a long way.

What do you get when all the giraffes leave work at once?
A giraffic jam.

If a tiger ran after you, what steps would you take?
Long ones!

Why are lions holy creatures?
They're always preying.

When is it safe to touch a lion?
When it's a dande-lion.

Why can't leopards escape from the zoo?
They're always spotted running away.

When can a horse leave the hospital and go home?
When it's in stable condition.

What do you call a chilly donkey?
A brrrr-o.

Who heads the Canine Mafia?
The Dogfather.

Why were the elephants thrown out of the lagoon?
They couldn't keep their trunks up.

What's the best way to get a rhino's attention?
Honk his horn.

Why are camels so hard to see?
They wear camel-flage.

In which month do beavers cut down trees?
Sep-timber.

Why do beavers love sequoia trees?
Because they're totally gnawsome.

What do you get when a hippopotamus plays in your room?

A hippopota-mess.

Why did the ram run off the cliff?
It missed the ewe turn.

What do you get when you cross a snake with a kangaroo?

A jump rope.

What kind of creatures live in banana trees?
Bananimals.

What do you do with a squeaky mouse?
Oil it.

Why should you rush a frog to the emergency room?
It could croak at any moment.

Where do sick kangaroos go?
To the hopsital.

What bird is always out of breath?
A puffin.

Which birds help build bridges?
Cranes.

What did the chickadee say when its bird feeder fell apart?

"Cheap, cheap."

Why did the bubblegum cross the road?

It was stuck on the chicken's foot.

Why did the dinosaur cross the road?

Chickens hadn't evolved yet.

3. Beach Bloopers

What do bumblebees wear on the beach?
Bee-kinis.

What do chickens collect on the beach?
Egg shells.

Why did Silly Sarah bring butter to the beach?
She heard it was toasty there.

What happens to a Barbie doll if you leave her out in the sun too long?
She gets Barbie-cued.

How does Santa squeeze into his swimsuit?
He holds his breadth.

What does a shark get when it swallows your computer?
A megabite.

OCEAN SPRAYS

What did the ocean say to the sand?
"How ya dune?"

What did the ocean say to the oyster?
"What time do you open up?"

What did the ocean say to the pier?
"There's something fishy going on here."

Where do goblins like to cruise?
From ghost to ghost.

What day of the week do fish hate most?
Fry-day.

What happened to the banana after it got sunburned?
Its skin peeled.

Why didn't Silly Sarah buy a larger bathing suit?
Because she'd be swimming in it.

Why did Silly Sarah carry lamps to the beach?
She wanted a good pair of shades.

Why don't elephants like the beach?
They always get sand in their trunks.

Why does Neptune carry a trident?
His fork is in the dishwasher.

How does Neptune keep his underwater castle clean?
He hires mer-maids.

SCUBA-DOO

Why do scuba divers say grace underwater?
Because they're so tank-ful.

What does Cinderella wear while scuba diving?
Glass flippers.

When do scuba divers sleep underwater?
When they're wearing their snore-kels.

What should you use if your scuba mask falls apart?
Masking tape.

Why can't whales keep secrets?
They're blubber-mouths.

Why do fish go after worms?
Because they're hooked on them.

What kind of fish growls?
A bear-acuda.

What kind of fish has two knees?
Two-knee fish.

Who should you call if you want to square dance on the beach?

The fiddler crabs.

Why did Silly Sarah feel safe swimming in the crocodile lagoon?

Because the sharks scared the gators away.

How did Silly Sarah get rescued from the undertow?

She dialed 911 on her shellular phone.

How do lobsters get to the airport?

By taxi crab.

What do carpenters read on the beach?

The Daily Sandpaper.

What do you get if your coconuts fall into the campfire?

Hot cocoa-nuts.

Why should you build a moat around your sandcastle?

For the moat-er boats.

What did the sandcastle say to the ocean wave?

"If you don't stop, my name will be mud."

What do rain clouds wear under their raincoats?

Thunderwear.

What do you call two witches who cruise together?
Broommates.

What happened after Sammy Seagull broke up with
Samantha Seagull?
He found a new gull-friend.

What do you call seagulls that fly over the bay?
Bagels.

4. Are We There Yet?

Why do elephants have trunks?
They'd look silly with suitcases on their faces.

What kind of car does a cow drive?
A Cattle-ac.

What kind of bus do fleas take on vacation?
A Greyhound.

PACK YOUR BAGGIES

What does the Sandman pack his clothes in?
A nap-sack.

What does a reporter pack her clothes in?
A paper bag.

What do boxers pack their clothes in?
Sluggage.

What do parachute jumpers pack their gear in?
Air bags.

How do you get down from a helicopter?
You don't get down from a helicopter. You get down from a duck.

What does a dragon do when he misses the train?
Dragon fly.

How can you tell if a train has just gone by?
You can see its tracks.

Why is a junk car like a baby?
It never goes anywhere without a rattle.

32

Why did the bus driver go broke?
He drove all his customers away.

Why did the little Volkswagen cry on the way to the repair shop?
It had to go where it was towed to.

What makes taxi cabs sweet and sticky?
Traffic jam.

What happened when Lady Godiva galloped to town?
She got there in time—barely.

What's the fastest way to get to the hospital?
Pick a fight with a dinosaur.

What does Tom do when he's driving to the movie studio?
Sets the Cruise control.

How does a duck change a flat tire?
With a quacker jack.

How do rabbits travel on vacation?
On TransWorld Hare-lines.

Where do working bees travel?
On buzzzzzzness trips.

Where do chickens go on vacation?
Sandy Egg-o.

Where do ducks go on vacation?
Alba-quacky, New Mexico.

Where do termites vacation?
In Holly-wood.

What country makes you shiver?
Chile.

What's purple and 5,000 miles long?
The Grape Wall of China.

What's the weather like in Mexico City?
Chili today and hot tamale.

What did Silly Sarah think of the Grand Canyon?
That it was just gorges.

Where are the Great Plains?
At the great airports.

What's black and white and lives in Bermuda?
A lost penguin.

What speaks every language?
An echo.

Why is the letter "t" like an island?
It's in the middle of water.

What keys won't fit in any door?
The Florida Keys.

Why was there a box of tissue in the hotel elevator?
It was coming down with something.

Why did Silly Billy spend his spring break in Iceland?
He wanted to see it before it melted.

What happens to a frog's car when the meter expires?
It gets toad away.

What do clowns do when they get into a car?
Chuckle-up.

Why was the auto mechanic fired?
He took too many brakes.

How does a kangaroo start its car if the battery's dead?
With jumper cables.

What did the jack say to the car?
"Need a lift?"

What kind of car starts with T?

Cars don't start with tea, they start with gas.

Why can't you fit into a carload of mushrooms?

There isn't mushroom inside.

What do you get when it rains on your convertible?

A carpool.

Where do old bicycle tires go?

To the old spokes home.

What happened when dinosaurs started driving?

They had tyrannosaurus wrecks.

Why was the bridesmaid arrested during the wedding?
For holding up a train.

Why did Silly Billy stare at the auto's radio?
He wanted to watch car tunes.

Why can't you take a bus home?
Your mom would make you return it.

When do frogs take a vacation?
In a leap year.

Where do chickens get off the highway?
At the eggs-it.

Where do lawnmowers fill up?
At the grass station.

5. Long Time, No Sea

What do you say to a skeleton going on a cruise?
"Bone Voyage!"

Why do birds fly south for the winter?
Because they can't afford a cruise.

Why can't hobos take boat trips?
Because beggars can't be cruisers.

Why can't you play cards on a cruise?
Because the passengers sit on all the decks.

What kind of lettuce do you get on an Alaskan cruise?
  Iceberg.

What does a pine tree wear on an Alaskan cruise?
  Its fir coat.

Why did the mummy go on a cruise?
  It needed a place to unwind.

Where do shellfish sleep on a cruise?
  In their crab-ins.

Why couldn't the elephant take a cruise?
  The airline lost its trunk.

Where does Tiger Woods take a cruise?
In the Golf of Mexico.

YO-HO-HO

Why do pirates have only one eye?
Because that's the way it's spelled.

Why do pirates work out at gyms?
To show off their big chests.

What's a pirate's favorite card game?
Rum-my.

Why aren't pirates allowed to compete in the
Olympics?
They only want the silver and gold.

What kind of pictures do sailors paint?
Watercolors.

Why do sailors use knots instead of miles?
They like to see the ocean tide.

When are sailors fired?
When the captain wants a crew-cut.

Why did the ship run over the channel marker?
It was a bad buoy.

What kind of ship can last forever?
Friend-ship.

If you try to cross the ocean in a leaky ship, what do you get?
About halfway.

What did Columbus do after he crossed the Atlantic?
Dried himself off.

What did Silly Billy say when the Statue of Liberty sneezed?

"God Bless America."

What do you get if the Three Blind Mice fall into the Arctic Ocean?

Mice cubes.

What do you call the tiny streams that flow into the Nile?

Juve-niles.

How can you tell the big waves from the little waves?

They wear white caps.

What is the national homeland for fish?

Fin-land.

6. Pucks & Yucks

When do hens play hockey?
When they have the chicken pucks.

Why can't centipedes skateboard?
They can't afford 100 knee pads.

Why are spiders good baseball players?
They catch lots of flies.

What do you win at the Arctic Olympics?
Cold medals.

How do scientists know cavemen played golf?
They always carried their clubs.

What would you do if you saw a catfish?
Help it hold the pole.

What's the difference between a football player and a duck?
One's in a huddle, the other's in a puddle.

Why don't fortune-tellers go bowling?
Crystal balls don't have finger-holes.

Why don't dinosaurs go bowling?
No one has size 3000X bowling shoes.

Why do basketball players have to wear bibs?
They dribble all over the court.

Why did the judge become a basketball player?
The court was bigger.

What does a basketball team do for breakfast?
Dunk donuts.

Who mows the grass at the ballpark?
A diamond cutter.

Why can't golfers attend college?
They can only count up to "Fore!"

Where do volleyball players go to dance?
To the beach ball.

What's the easiest way to catch a trout?
Have someone throw it to you.

Why can't fish play volleyball?
They won't go near the net.

Why didn't Noah do too much fishing on the ark?
He only had two worms.

Why can't Batman and Robin go fishing?
Robin eats all the worms.

Why did the football team have a baby ghost for a mascot?
It needed a little team spirit.

Why did Silly Billy think he'd do so well on the football team?
Because he had athlete's foot.

Why was the hockey player successful?
He always aimed for his goals.

WHAT'S THEIR GAME?

What's a baker's favorite game?
Pat-a-cake.

What's a sculptor's favorite game?
Marbles.

What's Mickey Mouse's favorite game?
Hide and Squeak.

What's Bill Gates's favorite game?
Monopoly.

What's a weatherman's favorite game?
Twister.

What's a ballet dancer's favorite game?
Tic-tac-toe.

What's a grocery clerk's favorite game?
Checkers.

What's a boxer's favorite part of a joke?
The punch line.

What does a karate expert wear to hold up his black pants?
His black belt.

Why was the martial arts expert sick?
He had Kung Flu.

What's small, white, and pumps iron?
Extra-strength aspirin.

What's a runner's favorite subject in school?
Jog-raphy.

Why aren't pigs allowed to play soccer?
They always hog the ball.

What do pitchers do when they get angry?
They throw tantrums.

Why does a pitcher raise one leg when he pitches?
If he raises both, he falls down.

Where does a catcher keep his mitt?
In the glove compartment.

Where does the catcher sit at the dinner table?
Behind the plate.

What did the glove say to the baseball?
"Catch you later!"

7. Fast Food Freak-Outs

What do vultures always have for dinner?
Leftovers.

What kind of bird is a gulp?
It's like a swallow, only bigger.

Where would you be if you had pepperoni and cheese in your hair?
Under the Leaning Tower of Pizza.

What should you do if you get chili in a Mexican restaurant?
Put on a sweater.

What should you do if there's tomato soup on the menu?

Wipe it off.

Why wouldn't the lobster share her lunch?

She was shellfish.

What do gophers do when they're hungry?

Gopher a pizza.

What do bees wear out to dinner?

Yellow jackets.

Why do dogs like to eat at Italian restaurants?
For the paws-ta.

Where can you leave your dog when you go into a restaurant?
In the barking lot.

What kind of snake loves dessert?
Pie-thons.

What's a rattlesnake's favorite holiday?
Fangs-giving.

What did the cannibal chef name his son?
Stew.

What do sharks eat at restaurants?
Fish and ships.

What's a cold puppy sitting on a rabbit?
A chili dog on a bun.

What did the duck say when it was finished eating?
"Put it on my bill."

What topping do anteaters order on their pizza?
Ant-chovies.

What cereal do skiers eat for breakfast?
Snow Flakes.

If a gown is evening wear, what's a suit of armor?
Silverware.

Why did the skunk call the restaurant?
So he could place his odor.

What's the best exercise to do while eating corn flakes?
Crunches.

Why do whales have big mouths?
So they can eat subs.

What does Jaws order at a restaurant?
Chef Salad.

What do skeletons order at restaurants?
Spare ribs.

What do you get when Dracula eats a sno-cone?
Frostbite.

Why can't you take a turkey out for dinner?
It gobbles its food.

What do cavemen eat for lunch?
A club sandwich.

Where do you bury turkey bones?
In the gravy yard.

Why did Silly Billy order a large plate of shellfish?
He wanted big mussels.

Why did Grumpy Gus eat at the seafood restaurant?
The sign said, "We Serve Crabs."

Where do spies buy their groceries?
At the snoopermarket.

How do you make a chocolate shake?
Take it to a scary movie.

What do ghosts put in their coffee?
Heavy scream.

How does a computer programmer order in a
restaurant?
From a pull-down menu.

Why should you carry cookies in each hand?
For balanced meals.

What does the Jolly Green Giant use to eat his beans?
A forklift.

Why should you eat grasshoppers and frogs?
Doctors say green things are good for you.

What happened to the computer programmer's cheese sandwich?

His mouse ate it.

What snack does the Easter Bunny leave in your navel?

Belly beans.

What do computer viruses eat for snacks?

Microchips.

Why did Silly Sarah put popcorn in her sneakers?

To feed her pigeon toes.

Why did Dracula's computer die?

He took a few bytes out of it.

8. Sym-phony

Why did Silly Sarah quit ballet class?
It was tutu hard.

Why are horses terrible dancers?
They have two left feet.

How do baby chicks dance?
Cheep-to-cheep.

Where does Tiger Woods go to dance?
The golf ball.

DANCE WITH ME

What kind of dancing do pirates love?
The rum-ba.

What kind of dancing do telephone repairmen love?
Line dancing.

What kind of dancing do geometry teachers love?
Square dancing.

What kind of dancing do owls love?
The whoo-la.

Where do rabbits go to hear singing?
The hopera.

Who are the cleanest opera singers?
Soap-ranos.

Why was the opera singer arrested?
She was always breaking into song.

Who sings slightly lower than a tenor?
A niner.

Why did the stage manager put paste on the programs?
So the audience would be glued to their seats.

Why did Friar Tuck buy a trumpet?
Robin Hood asked him to join his band.

Why did they let the turkey join the band?
He had the drumsticks.

Where do hurricanes sit during band practice?
In the wind section.

What instrument do lighthouse keepers play?

Fog horns.

Where do pigs play their violins?

In the pork-estra.

What happens to a harp when its strings break?

It has open-harp surgery.

Why did the shy conductor stand with his back to the orchestra?

He couldn't face the music.

What's an orchestra conductor's favorite dessert?

Cello pudding.

What instrument do dogs love to play?
The trom-bone.

What instrument do proud Scotsmen play?
Bragpipes.

What do Scottish people put in their VCRs?
Scotch tapes.

What music do baby bees like?
A Bee CD.

Why should you study your music lesson before crossing a busy street?

If you don't C-sharp, you will B-flat.

When you go to the movie theater, do you need supervision?

No, regular vision will do.

Why couldn't Ms. Skunk get into the movie theater?

She was ten scents short.

What's a chicken's favorite movie rental store?

Bok-bok-bok-buster.

Why was the movie star ordered off the set?

He was acting up and making a scene.

What did Sir Lancelot do when he sat next to Lady Guinevere?

He put his armor round her.

What did the famous movie star dog do after its performance?

Took a bow-wow.

Why was the actor ordered off the set of *Gladiator*?

He couldn't remember his lions.

9. Awful Authors

What's the best way to communicate with a trout?
Drop it a line.

Why did the milk carton sleep in the library?
It wanted to curdle up with a good book.

What did the pencil say to the paper?
"I dot my I's on you."

Why should you take a pen to the garden?
So you can weed and write.

Is it bad to write on an empty stomach?
  No, but it's better to write on paper.

Why did Silly Sarah crawl into her math class?
  The teacher told her never to walk in late again.

What should you do if your baby brother is chewing up your favorite book?
  Take the words right out of his mouth.

What did the librarian use for bait?
  A bookworm.

Which letters of the alphabet have wings?
  Bs and Js.

Why was Silly Sarah sad after a half-day of school?
  Because the other half was after lunch.

What's the longest sentence in the world?
  "Life imprisonment."

Why was Silly Billy afraid to go to school?
  He had class-trophobia.

What's a seal's favorite subject at school?
  Art, art!

What's the only word in the dictionary always pronounced incorrectly?

Incorrectly.

What's a dog called that runs a book company?

A pup-lisher.

Why was the polar bear upset with her test grade?

It was 20 below zero.

What's filled with ink and has no hair?

A bald-point pen.

Where do you go to take a class in making desserts?

Sundae school.

What knight writes at a round table?
King Author.

When does seven come before six?
In the dictionary.

What word has the most letters in it?
Mailbox.

How do dogs like going to school?
They have a ruff time.

What do you call a teacher who makes numbers disappear?
A mathemagician.

What's a teacher's favorite food?

Graded cheese.

How do you e-mail a fish?

Get it online.

How do wasps communicate on their computers?

By bee-mail.

When composing a term paper, what side of your brain do you use?

The write brain.

What did the pen say to the pencil?

"So what's your point?"

Why did Silly Billy stare at his grandmother?
The teacher told him to study his grammar.

Why did the computer squeak?
Someone stepped on its mouse.

What kind of puzzles do toads like?
Crosswarts.

Which animal is smarter than a talking parrot?
A spelling bee.

What do plants in your math class grow?
Square roots.

How did the lettuce get an A on the test?
It used its head.

Why does your teacher wear sunglasses?
Because her class is so bright.

What should you do if you get a B on your math test?
Be careful it doesn't sting you.

10. People Patter

Where do polar bears invest their money?
In snowbanks.

Who uses voodoo to scare mosquitoes away?
The itch doctor.

Why did the forest ranger change jobs?
He wanted to turn over a new leaf.

What's a garage mechanic's favorite exercise?
Jumping jacks.

What do you get when you cross a pit bull with a math teacher?

Snappy answers.

MAD ABOUT YOU

Did you hear about the angry clockmaker?
She was ticked off.

Did you hear about the angry cloned scientist?
He was beside himself.

Did you hear about the angry kangaroo?
It was hopping mad.

Did you hear about the angry bull?
It saw red.

Did you hear about the angry golfer?
She was teed off.

Why was the king only 12 inches tall?
He was the ruler of his country.

How does a scientist get ready for work?
He puts his genes on.

What's a couch potato's favorite TV show?
"M.A.S.H."

What exam must vegetarian lawyers pass before they can practice law?
The salad bar.

What did the lawyer name her daughter?
Sue.

What kind of uniforms do paratroopers wear?
Jump suits.

What did the weatherman say to the grocer?
"I'll take a rain check."

What did the princess say when her photos didn't arrive?
"Someday my prints will come."

Who is the sacred woman of Tibet?
The Dalai Mama.

What kind of doctor treats ducks?
A quack.

Why are police officers like shirtmakers?
They're always making collars.

Why do cats make excellent maids?
They enjoy a little light mousekeeping.

What's a private detective's favorite vegetable?
A cluecumber.

What does the Lone Ranger use to make up his eyes?
Mask-ara.

Why do undertakers cremate bodies?
To urn their living.

What do garage mechanics wear to ballet class?
Tow shoes.

Where do baby computer programmers like to sit?
On your laptop.

Why do store clerks pack T-shirts in boxes?
Because teabags are too small.

If carpenters measure with yardsticks, what do sailors measure with?
Fishsticks.

Where did Indiana Jones find dinosaur eggs?
On an eggspedition.

What kind of shoes do spies wear?
Sneakers.

What knight never won a battle?
  Sir Ender.

What did Silly Billy say to his mean dentist?
  "You really hurt my fillings."

What does a butcher weigh?
  Meat!

Who invented spaghetti?
  Someone who used his noodle.

What do lawyers wear to court?
  Lawsuits.

What do you get when you cross your right eye with
your left eye?
  Dizzy.

11. Garden Goofies

What vegetable do chickens grow in their gardens?
Eggplant.

Why should you bury your money in the garden?
To make the soil rich.

What's a ghost's favorite plant?
Bam-BOO!

What flowers grow right under your nose?
Tulips.

Why are May flowers so clean?
From all the April showers.

What holiday do cornstalks celebrate every summer?
Happy New Ear.

What does a worm do in a cornfield?
Goes in one ear and out the other.

What fruit is always in a bad mood?
The crab apple.

How do you fix a pumpkin?
With a pumpkin patch.

What vegetable do you get when a dinosaur tromps through your garden?
Squash.

What comes after cucumbers?
R-cumbers.

What's the most environmentally safe fuel?
Aspara-gas.

What happened when Mama Rabbit was chased out of the farmer's garden?
She didn't carrot all.

Where do vegetables go to get married?
To the Justice of the Peas.

What do vegetables give each other when they get married?
Onion rings.

Did all the animals go into Noah's Ark in pairs?
No, the worms went in apples.

What do you call spiders that just got married?
Newlywebs.

Why did the grapefruit fall in love with the banana?
The banana had ap-peel.

Why did the grapefruit stop rolling?
It ran out of juice.

What do most people think about the centers of cherries?
They're the pits.

What did the snail say when it hitched a ride on a turtle?
"Wheee!"

What does Santa do in his garden?
Hoe-hoe-hoe.

What do frogs think of your garden?
That it's toadally awesome.

Which garden insects are always polite?
Lady bugs.

Why should lightning bugs apply to college?
Because they're very bright.

Which organizations do little plants join?
The Boy Sprouts and the Girl Sprouts.

What kind of monkeys are found in flower gardens?
Chim-pansies.

What kind of bees are found in dead flower gardens?
Zom-bees.

What did the spider say to the moth?
"Please stick around for dinner."

What do garden snakes do after a fight?
Hiss and make up.

Why are gardeners good quilters?
They like to sow.

Why do quilters love pine trees?
They're full of needles.

How can you recognize a dogwood tree?
By its bark.

How do trees like their ice cream served?
In a pine cone.

What evergreen tree shoots its needles?
A porcu-pine.

12. Knock-Knocks

Knock-knock.
Who's there?
Arthur.
Arthur who?
Arthur mometer says it's
120 degrees!

Knock-knock.
Who's there?
Sherwood.
Sherwood who?
Sherwood like you to
come to the beach.

Knock-knock.
Who's there?
Pecan.
Pecan who?
Pecan someone your own size.

Knock-knock.
  Who's there?
Senior.
  Senior who?
Senior hockey stick
around here lately?

Knock-knock.
  Who's there?
Hyena.
  Hyena who?
Hyena tree I saw a
monkey.

Knock-knock.
  Who's there?
Canoe.
  Canoe who?
Canoe help me take this
fish off my line?

Knock-knock.
  Who's there?
Dozen.
  Dozen who?
Dozen anybody want
this last pickle?

Knock-knock.
  Who's there?
Ketchup.
  Ketchup who?
Ketchup to her before
she skates into that
dumpster!

Knock-knock.
   Who's there?
Roxanne.
   Roxanne who?
Roxanne shells were
scattered all over the
beach.

Knock-knock.
   Who's there?
Annapolis.
   Annapolis who?
Annapolis what you eat
every day to keep the
doctor away.

Knock-knock.
   Who's there?
Amos.
   Amos who?
Amos quito bit me on the
arm.

Knock-knock.
   Who's there?
Sweden.
   Sweden who?
Sweden my lemonade
with some sugar,
will you?

Knock-knock.
   Who's there?
Iran.
   Iran who?
Iran all the way to third
base.

Knock-knock.
Who's there?
Allowed.
Allowed who?
Allowed person isn't
welcome in the library.

Knock-knock.
Who's there?
Norma Lee.
Norma Lee who?
Norma Lee I don't go to
the beach without my
pail.

Knock-knock.
Who's there?
Rhoda.
Rhoda who?
Rhoda boat across the
lake by myself.

Knock-knock.
Who's there?
Charlotte.
Charlotte who?
Charlotte of mosquitoes
out tonight.

Knock-knock.
Who's there?
Dishes.
Dishes who?
Dishes me. Who ish you?

Knock-knock.
Who's there?
Siena.
Siena who?
Siena good movies lately?

Knock-knock.
Who's there?
Distress.
Distress who?
Distress makes me look
too fat.

Knock-knock.
Who's there?
Lady.
Lady who?
Lady tablecloth down on
the picnic table first.

Knock-knock.
Who's there?
Sadie.
Sadie who?
Sadie word "please" and
you can eat dessert first.

Knock-knock.
Who's there?
Les.
Les who?
Les go for a swim before
we eat.

Knock-knock.

Who's there?

Lionel.

Lionel who?

Lionel bite your hand if you stick it in the cage.

Knock-knock.

Who's there?

Diana.

Diana who?

Diana thirst . . . can I have some lemonade?

Knock-knock.

Who's there?

Daisy.

Daisy who?

Daisy plays, nights he sleeps.

Knock-knock.

Who's there?

Douglas.

Douglas who?

Douglas broke when I poured lemonade in it.

Knock-knock.
Who's there?
Dragon.
Dragon who?
Dragon your feet will
only make Dad angry.

Knock-knock.
Who's there?
Throat.
Throat who?
Throat to me,
and I'll catch it.

Knock-knock.
Who's there?
Thumb.
Thumb who?
Thumb like it hot,
thumb like it cold.

Knock-knock.
Who's there?
Turnip.
Turnip who?
Turnip the TV,
I can't hear it.

Knock-knock.
Who's there?
Tennis.
Tennis who?
Tennis five plus
three plus two.

Knock-knock.
  Who's there?
Juliet.
  Juliet who?
Juliet a huge slice of
watermelon.

Knock-knock.
  Who's there?
Doris.
  Doris who?
Doris locked—that's why I
knocked!

Knock-knock.
  Who's there?
Tooth.
  Tooth who?
Tooth company,
threeth a crowd.

Knock-knock.
  Who's there?
Police.
  Police who?
Police let me in . . .
it's raining out here!

Knock-knock.
  Who's there?
Annie.
  Annie who.
Annie body home?

Knock-knock.
  Who's there?
Izzy.
  Izzy who?
Izzy coming or isn't he?

Knock-knock.

  Who's there?

Thermos.

  Thermos who?

Thermos be a better knock-knock than this one.

Knock-knock.

  Who's there?

Thistle.

  Thistle who?

Thistle be the last knock-knock in the book.

INDEX

94